CONTEMPLATING
THE FACE OF CHRIST

CONTEMPLATING THE FACE OF CHRIST

A WAY OF THE CROSS

By Marko Ivan Rupnik, SJ

Translated by Mary Leonora Wilson, FSP

Pauline
BOOKS & MEDIA
Boston

Nihil Obstat: Reverend Thomas W. Buckley, S.T.D., S.S.L.

Imprimatur: ✠ Seán Cardinal O'Malley, O.F.M. Cap.
Archbishop of Boston
June 15, 2017

Originally published in Italian as *Via Crucis* by Marko Ivan Rupnik, SJ. Photos of Marko Ivan Rupnik's art © Centro Aletti Via Paolina, 25- 00184, Rome, Italy. All rights reserved.

ISBN 10: 0-8198-1669-8

ISBN 13: 978-0-8198-1669-6

Cover design by Rosana Usselmann

Cover and interior art by Marko Ivan Rupnik, S.J.

Published by Pauline Books & Media, 50 Saint Pauls Avenue, Boston, MA 02130-3491

Printed in the U.S.A.

www.pauline.org

Pauline Books & Media is the publishing house of the Daughters of St. Paul, an international congregation of women religious serving the Church with the communications media.

1 2 3 4 5 6 7 8 9   22 21 20 19 18

FOREWORD

Mosaic reigned throughout the Mediter-
ranean as Christianity's highest art form for
almost a thousand years. Apses, chapels, tombs,
and reliquaries were adorned with the dazzling
effect of tiny tiles united to form images. The small
parts becoming a beautiful whole, the time-
consuming care and the loving craftsmanship that
comprise the art of mosaic, rendered the very
medium itself an expression of man's cooperation
with the divine. However, the effect of these shim-
mering skins of glass or stone was its greatest
power, evoking for rich and poor alike a transcen-
dent vision of beauty. The majestic figures standing
against their eternal backgrounds could be prayed
before by aristocrat or slave. Neither status nor

wealth mattered in front of the glorious saints robed in color and light, which reminded everyone of those who were always listening beyond the church walls.

Despite many centuries of mosaic masters before him, Father Marko Ivan Rupnik has succeeded in infusing new contemporary energy into this ancient artistic language. His essential forms with their clear outlines lend the immediacy of the Baroque without the distraction of ornamentation. The tiles, assembled and chosen with the same care as the craftsmen of Ravenna and Constantinople, alternate between broad and minute, creating a poetic cadence to his surfaces, and Rupnik's colors shift from the calm matte of stone to the kinetic hues of enamel. Within the simplicity of the forms, the detail of the work allows for an even deeper level of meditation on the scenes before us.

But it is the holy faces portrayed by Rupnik that captivate the viewer. Large, round heads with enormous eyes, which seem to be truly all-seeing, translate the power of modern cinema to this most antique art. Rupnik's faces fill the frame; Jesus' massive, dark eyes seem to absorb everything around them, even when he is crushed by his giant cross. When Christ's eyes close at his death, the energy leaves the scene and the viewer feels bereft.

Father Rupnik's revival of the art of mosaic comes at a critical moment in cultural history. The dense compositions of the Renaissance are hard for the modern faithful to follow: the complicated histories and myriad artistic references no longer resonate as they once did. But by enhancing the ancient pious practice of the Stations of the Cross with images that draw us alongside Christ—Godlike in his luminosity, yet vulnerable in his humanity—Father Rupnik opens a window into Christ's passion where art becomes comprehensible and engaging for all and clearly at the service of prayer.

ELIZABETH LEV

INTRODUCTION

The Way of the Cross is the most familiar and popular form of devotion there is to the Passion of Christ. We pray the Way of the Cross to contemplate Christ's suffering and to move ourselves to compassion. The stations are the last link in a long series of devotional practices that have developed over time. Pilgrimages to the Holy Land began as early as the fourth century. Calvary and the Holy Sepulcher became the destinations of special processions which, over time, spread to other places made holy by the Lord's sufferings.

In the Middle Ages, Saint Francis' live crèche[*] gave a strong impetus to a spirituality of the image

---

[*] Saint Bonaventure recounted that Saint Francis, a few years before his death, set up a live manger scene in a village town square in Italy and preached about the miracle of Christmas and the poor king who was born in a manger.

and, consequently, to evangelization. Francis saw the nativity scene as a way for the faithful to identify with the moods, feelings, and thoughts of the characters involved in the birth of Jesus. This produced a much more integral and complex approach than that of mere verbal proclamation. Because salvation is brought about by the Word Incarnate, the Son of God made man, it must necessarily involve the whole person. Only then can it fully propose and produce a way of life that makes us contemporaries of Christ and of the events of salvation. Therefore, a scene is not simply a representation, because even at the Passion of Christ many people were present, yet they did not recognize Jesus as the Son of God and Savior of humanity.* Instead the scene is an image formed by the Word of God and by a great theological tradition.

A few centuries later, well into the modern age, Saint Ignatius of Loyola reaffirmed the importance of spiritual imagery. In the Spiritual Exercises,

---

* In other words, the scene is not simply a snapshot of a moment in time, but a way of proclaiming the Gospel through art so as to draw people to faith. —Ed.

Ignatius encourages retreatants to use their imagination for spiritual benefit. Within the essential theological framework, retreatants engage more fully with all their capacities and are set on fire for the Lord. For Ignatius, spiritual gain does not come from developing fanciful imaginings but from the intimate knowledge of God, who inflames us with His own love.

Our day seems especially suited to reclaim this tradition, which combines theology, art, and spirituality. Art makes visible the reality—the flesh—of the Word and of our faith. It also makes us partakers of the mystery that Gregory Nazianzen reminds us is like "drops of blood" that fall into the large chalice of the earth, "renewing the entire universe."

The images in this book are from a Way of the Cross outside the church of Santa Maria in Tolmin, Slovenia, on the crest of the Julian Alps. The stations were originally constructed after World War I, a war that caused so much suffering in that area. The suffering did not end but continued during World War II and later under communism, when the town, which borders Italy, became part of Yugoslavia. During that era, the Way of the Cross was destroyed. Years later the parish priest, Father Milan Sirk, wanted this mountain, which had seen so much violence, to have the Stations of the Cross once again. He commissioned Father Marko Rupnik and the artists from The Atelier of the Aletti Center for this work. They completed it in 2008.

In these mosaic portrayals of the Way of the Cross we see only glimpses of faces and flashes of eyes. All of the art's spiritual intensity is concentrated in Christ's face and gaze, since the face reveals the person. Excerpts from Sacred Scripture and ancient Christian writings accompany the images.

One might imagine that the Way of the Cross, with its unique richness, is a devotion typical of the West. However, the liturgical and theological roots of this devotion spring from the heart of the Christian mystery. The quotations highlight how Christians have contemplated this mystery from the very beginning.

FIRST STATION

JESUS IS
CONDEMNED
TO DEATH

℣. We adore you, O Christ,
and we bless you.

℟. Because by your holy cross
you have redeemed the world.

Now Jesus stood before the governor; and the governor asked him, "Are you the King of the Jews?" Jesus said, "You say so." But when he was accused by the chief priests and elders, he did not answer. Then Pilate said to him, "Do you not hear how many accusations they make against you?" But he gave him no answer, not even to a single charge, so that the governor was greatly amazed.

Matthew 27:11–14

After the first sin, which contaminated everything, human reason was wounded and subject to ignorance. We can fully grasp the truth only in communion with the One who is truth. Truth is sought in communion, because Truth *is* Communion (see Jn 14:6). We can't know truth without love, but sin destroyed love—that is, truth —in us. As a result, we created our own truth— the fruit of our own imaginations. Enclosed in our own little world, we became slaves of our own passions, leaving no space for God.

Thus, the face of Christ is hidden. Pilate looks into the eyes of Christ, but he does not see the truth (see Mt 4:12). The high priest Caiaphas directs his gaze elsewhere. He follows his own religious schemes, which prevent him from recognizing the Lord in that face so close to him. But neither thought, nor the law, nor human strength can see or recognize God, because God is love. Love is personal; it has a face. And it's not enough to just recognize a face. We need to see in it the face of God—the God who loves every man and woman.

This meek face of Christ becomes a place of encounter for those who are judged and condemned. In it they welcome the meekness and compassion of the One who was judged unjustly. Since judgment belongs to God alone, those who judge separate themselves from God. But if they contemplate this meek and good face, the gaze of the Judged One will embrace them too. He takes upon Himself even their condemnation.

The Mighty One remained mute, the Word without words. Had he raised his voice, he would not have been conquered and he would not have ended on the cross, but neither would he have saved Adam. Thus, to suffer, he who confounded the wise with his wisdom conquered by not opening his mouth.

Romanus the Melodist,
Kontakion on the Passion

. . . He had no form or majesty that we should look
   at him,
      nothing in his appearance that we should
         desire him.
He was despised and rejected by others;
      a man of suffering and acquainted with
         infirmity;
and as one from whom others hide their faces
      he was despised, and we held him of no
         account.

Isaiah 53:2b–3

At the cross her station keeping
stood the mournful mother weeping,
close to Jesus to the last.

SECOND STATION

JESUS TAKES UP HIS CROSS

℣. We adore you, O Christ,
and we bless you.

℟. Because by your holy cross
you have redeemed the world.

So they took Jesus; and carrying the cross by himself, he went out to what is called The Place of the Skull, which in Hebrew is called Golgotha. There they crucified him, and with him two others, one on either side, with Jesus between them. Pilate also had an inscription written and put on the cross. It read, "Jesus of Nazareth, the King of the Jews."

John 19:16b–19

Christ shoulders the cross. His strong hands take the cross carefully, almost as if the heavy wood were itself wounded humanity, needing God's attention and care. Therefore Christ embraces the cross, placing His face against it tenderly. His embrace demonstrates God's loving response to what is evil in humanity. The Passion begins to unfold more explicitly in this moment: the New Adam, immune from sin, identifies Himself with the old, sinful Adam, absorbing the old Adam's sinfulness. By accepting the cross, Christ voluntarily takes upon himself all of humanity, even its sin and the wages of sin: death.

We no longer have to go back and look for our sins in the place where we committed them or search our memory; instead we find them in the cross upon Christ's shoulders. As sinners, we begin to heal when we feel the tenderness of the Savior's hands on our wounds and aching flesh, when we fix our gaze on Him who has taken our sin upon Himself. We are freed from sin when our eyes are fixed on the Savior and His cross.

When blessed Abraham ascended the mountain that God had shown him, so that there he might sacrifice Isaac according to God's command, he laid the wood upon the boy. Isaac, carrying his own cross upon his shoulders, prefigured Christ going up to the glory of his passion. Christ taught us that his passion was his glory, saying, "Now is the Son of man glorified, and God is glorified in him. If God be glorified in him, God will also glorify him in himself, and will immediately glorify him" (Jn 13:31–32).

Cyril of Alexandria,
Commentary on Luke

The Word became "bearer of the flesh" so that men might become "bearers of the Spirit."

Athanasius of Alexandria,
On the Incarnation

He was oppressed, and he was afflicted,
>	yet he did not open his mouth;
like a lamb that is led to the slaughter,
>	and like a sheep that before its shearers is silent,
>	so he did not open his mouth.

Isaiah 53:7

Through her heart, his sorrow sharing,
all his bitter anguish bearing,
now at length the sword had passed.

Third Station

JESUS FALLS
THE FIRST TIME

℣. We adore you, O Christ,
and we bless you.

℟. Because by your holy cross
you have redeemed the world.

The next day [John] saw Jesus coming toward him and declared, "Here is the Lamb of God who takes away the sin of the world! This is he of whom I said, 'After me comes a man who ranks ahead of me because he was before me.'"

John 1:29–30

With that same expression on His face, veiled by a touch of sadness, Christ "listens" to the cross. Placing His head against it, He hears its narrative, the story of the world's evil. Only the Creator knows the endless abysses of sin that we, created in the image of God, are capable of entering with our free will. Only He, the Redeemer, can take upon Himself that evil caused by choices separated from love. With an egoistic focus on self and a will severed from love, we pervert the truth of our being made in the image of God. Then our identity begins to be more clearly and decisively carved like a sin-laden cross.

Christ freely enters into the tragic course of human history and gathers up every individual's "cross of sin." The Lamb of God has piled the sins of the world upon Himself. But to gather every last one of them, He Himself descends, falling, to lay His ear on the remotest sufferings and on the worst sins carried out in the hidden abysses of darkness.

———— ○◄►○ ————

Because of his ardent love for creation, God the Father surrendered his own Son to death on the cross. . . . This was not, however, because he could not redeem us in another way, but because he wanted the manifestation of his overflowing love to *be a teacher to us*. And through the death of his only begotten Son, he drew us closer to himself. Yes, if he had possessed anything more precious, he would have given it to us, so that by it our race might become his own. Because of his great love he did *not* will to do violence to our freedom, even though he could easily have done so. Instead, he preferred that we draw near him by the love of our understanding. Because of his love for us and out of obedience to his Father, Christ joyously accepted insults and bitterness. . . . In the same way, when saints become perfect they all reach this perfection, and by abundantly pouring out their love and their compassion on all mankind they resemble God.

Isaac the Syrian,
First Collection

Surely he has borne our infirmities
     and carried our diseases;
yet we accounted him stricken,
     struck down by God, and afflicted.
But he was wounded for our transgressions,
     crushed for our iniquities;
upon him was the punishment that made us whole,
     and by his bruises we are healed.

Isaiah 53:4–5

Oh, how sad and sore distressed
was that Mother highly blest
of the sole-begotten one!

FOURTH STATION

JESUS MEETS HIS MOTHER

℣. We adore you, O Christ,
and we bless you.

℟. Because by your holy cross
you have redeemed the world.

And the child's father and mother were amazed at what was being said about him. Then Simeon blessed them and said to his mother, Mary, "This child is destined for the falling and the rising of many in Israel, and to be a sign that will be opposed so that the inner thoughts of many will be revealed—and a sword will pierce your own soul too."

Luke 2:33–35

On the way of the cross, Jesus meets His Mother. Mary, more than anyone, sees what is happening through the eyes of her Son. Love allows us to see a situation as God does. Mary welcomed and fulfilled the work of the Holy Spirit to the point that the Word became incarnate in her. It is only in harmony and cooperation with the Holy Spirit that we can see our reality and everything we have experienced in relation to, or better still, *in* Christ.

Unless our gaze meets His, suffering and pain can become a temptation to which we succumb. Only love manages to unite us so fundamentally with Christ that we can see our destiny in His abused and suffering body. Even more, we can comprehend the sense in which He changed evil into good. To become "Christ-formed" in suffering enables us to see good where no one else can find it.

Mary continues to acquire the wisdom of the cross, of the sword that pierces her heart (see Lk 2:35). She understands the salvific meaning of suffering, failure, and death. Her external eye may see a man afflicted and humiliated to the point of

death, but her interior eye, united to Christ, sees the transfiguration of an abyss.

Mary, the lamb, seeing her own Lamb led to slaughter, followed him with the other women and, consumed with grief, cried out: "Where are you going, my Son? For whom are you running so swiftly? Is there another wedding in Cana, and are you in a hurry to get there, to turn their water into wine? Shall I go with you, my Son, or shall I rather wait for you? Speak some word to me, O Word; do not pass me by in silence, O you who preserved me undefiled, for you are my Son and God."

Byzantine liturgy,
Office of the Holy Passion, *Kontakion*

You will be struck by the blade of uncertainty and your thoughts will tear you to pieces when you see him. He whom you heard called the Son of God, and knew to be begotten without the intervention of man, you will see crucified, at the point of death, subjected to human torture. You knew that at the end he lamented, "Father, if it is possible, let this chalice pass from me." [. . .] A sword will pierce your very soul.

Origen,
Homilies on Luke

Yet it was you who took me from the womb;
>   you kept me safe on my mother's breast.
On you I was cast from my birth,
>   and since my mother bore me you have been my
>   God.
Do not be far from me,
>   for trouble is near
>   and there is no one to help.

Psalm 22:9–11

Christ above in torment hangs,
she beneath beholds the pangs
of her dying, glorious Son.

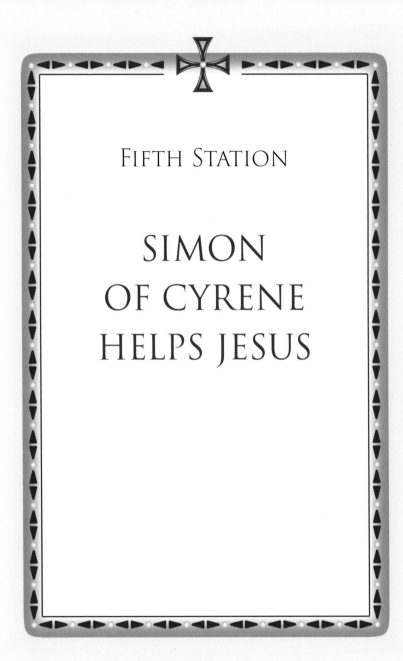

FIFTH STATION

SIMON
OF CYRENE
HELPS JESUS

℣. We adore you, O Christ,
and we bless you.

℟. Because by your holy cross
you have redeemed the world.

They compelled a passer-by, who was coming in from the country, to carry his cross; it was Simon of Cyrene, the father of Alexander and Rufus. Then they brought Jesus to the place called Golgotha (which means the place of a skull).

Mark 15:21–22

In a way the cross is a symbol of the evil and death that have come close to man because of sin. Yet for many, the cross remains something impersonal and distant. What it symbolizes—every human pain and suffering—also remains distant. Precisely in the process of defending ourselves from pain, we add still more pain and the cross becomes heavier. In reality, it is not the crosses that are important, but those who are crucified. To carry another's cross for a short while is not so difficult. The important thing is not to end up nailed to it.

But slowly our point of view changes when we realize that the Crucified is He who carries the cross of all humanity, He who will be nailed to it in our stead. Then everything begins to conform itself to Him. We can even welcome suffering and accept evil, but only when we are in a strong and experienced relationship with Christ. We must be so intensely in love as to seek to take up the cross as He took it up. Then we carry the cross for part of the way, knowing that at the end He will ascend it. He will be nailed and crucified, so that I may no

longer be crushed by my cross and by the evil done to me or that I have inflicted on others.

According to ancient tradition, Simon of Cyrene represents a great transformation. Instead of being one who is forced, he becomes one who embraces. This is the parable of Christian life: from slavery to the freedom of children, from obligation to willing acceptance. Redemption is not a yoke. Neither is it an imposition or an automatic process. It is the gift of a love that is free, that can only be answered by unconditional acceptance.

It was fitting not only for the Savior to take up his cross but that we carry it as well, thus fulfilling an arduous service, which for us is a source of salvation.

Origen,
Commentary on Matthew

It is for your sake that I have borne reproach,
that shame has covered my face.

I have become a stranger to my kindred,
    an alien to my mother's children.
It is zeal for your house that has consumed me;
        the insults of those who insult you have fallen
        on me.

Psalm 69:7–9

Is there one who would not weep,
whelmed in miseries so deep,
Christ's dear Mother to behold?

SIXTH STATION

VERONICA
WIPES THE FACE
OF JESUS

℣. We adore you, O Christ,
and we bless you.

℟. Because by your holy cross
you have redeemed the world.

Above all, maintain constant love for one another, for love covers a multitude of sins. Be hospitable to one another without complaining. Like good stewards of the manifold grace of God, serve one another with whatever gift each of you has received. Whoever speaks must do so as one speaking the very words of God; whoever serves must do so with the strength that God supplies, so that God may be glorified in all things through Jesus Christ.

1 Peter 4:8–11

In a gesture of tenderness, Veronica wipes Jesus' face free of blood, sweat, and spittle. The image of the holy Face remains imprinted on her veil. Love renders us similar to God because God is love. Veronica is the image of a woman moved by compassion, a sensitivity that reminds us of God. The veil that she used for her act of charity toward Christ becomes her new garment; she clothes herself with Christ. The image of God within her breaks through her body, through all that she is, and becomes visible in her gestures, in the way she moves, in her ways of thinking and acting.

In a certain sense, Veronica becomes the Gospel, that is, an icon of Christ. She becomes the model of the new woman, of the redeemed woman, because she is involved in Christ's redemption of the world. Her gesture becomes a symbol of spiritual cleansing. Veronica wipes the face of Christ and she is the one cleansed, clothed in the likeness of Christ, in whose image she is made. Charity is not about satisfying ourselves. Charity renders us divine. It is not we who "do charity." The charity of God molds us, cleanses us, and clothes us with

glory. The charity of God that we embrace does good in us.

Nothing disposes us more toward justice or . . . deification and resemblance to God as does compassion, which the soul carries with piety and joy to those in need. Indeed, the Word pointed out that the one who is in need of being helped is like God: "That which you do to one of these little ones"— he said—"you do to me" (Mt 25:40).

Maximus the Confessor,
Mystagogy

It is well with those who deal generously and lend,
    who conduct their affairs with justice.
For the righteous will never be moved;
    they will be remembered for ever.
They are not afraid of evil tidings;
    their hearts are firm, secure in the LORD.
Their hearts are steady, they will not be afraid;
    in the end they will look in triumph on their
        foes.

They have distributed freely, they have given to the
  poor;
     their righteousness endures for ever;
     their horn is exalted in honor.

Psalm 112:5–9

Can the human heart refrain
From partaking in her pain,
In that Mother's pain untold?

SEVENTH STATION

JESUS FALLS THE SECOND TIME

℣. We adore you, O Christ,
   and we bless you.

℟. Because by your holy cross
   you have redeemed the world.

The creation itself will be set free from its bondage to decay and will obtain the freedom of the glory of the children of God. We know that the whole creation has been groaning in labor pains until now; and not only the creation, but we ourselves, who have the first fruits of the Spirit, groan inwardly while we wait for adoption, the redemption of our bodies.

Romans 8:21–23

In Christ's second fall we contemplate the intensity and power of the love of the Lord, who lies prostrate in the dust. The cross and the weight of evil almost seem to have won. But in reality our Savior embraces the crushing burden of evil to reach into the very last pit where evil could have burrowed itself. His hand touches the ground, His intense gaze is focused and penetrating, and His ear rests against the dirt. Everything in Christ seeks to hear and to extract the sorrowful story of the earth soaked in the blood first shed by Cain, and then by his descendants even until the end of the world.

Silently, the merciful God gathers the earth's confession of evil. Once again, the earth hears the breath of God, the faint blowing, His hand again at work remolding and regenerating the new man. Only this time the dust will be mixed with the blood of the Lord. He expects those reborn by the Resurrection to collaborate in the cosmic event of the eighth day. Their present sufferings, like birth pains, will help to bring forth the new heaven and earth. The cross presses Christ to the ground and

imprints upon the material world a seal of love on all that God created and now redeems.

By being crucified, the Son of God left his imprint on the universe in the form of a cross, sealing in a way the entire universe with the sign of the cross.

Irenaeus of Lyons,
Proof of the Apostolic Preaching

The cross is the seal and mold of created things; in length and breadth, according to its form, everything is sealed.

Ephrem the Syrian,
Hymns on the Faith

I am poured out like water,
    and all my bones are out of joint;
my heart is like wax;
    it is melted within my breast;
my mouth is dried up like a potsherd,

and my tongue sticks to my jaws;
you lay me in the dust of death.

Psalm 22:14–15

Bruised, derided, cursed, defiled,
she beheld her tender child,
all with bloody scourges rent.

EIGHTH STATION

THE WOMEN
OF JERUSALEM
WEEP OVER JESUS

℣. We adore you, O Christ,
and we bless you.

℟. Because by your holy cross
you have redeemed the world.

A great number of the people followed him, and among them were women who were beating their breasts and wailing for him. But Jesus turned to them and said, "Daughters of Jerusalem, do not weep for me, but weep for yourselves and for your children. For the days are surely coming when they will say, 'Blessed are the barren, and the wombs that never bore, and the breasts that never nursed.' Then they will begin to say to the mountains, 'Fall on us'; and to the hills, 'Cover us.' For if they do this when the wood is green, what will happen when it is dry?"

Luke 23:27–31

Christ's passage through the crowd on the way to Calvary provokes people to react in different ways. The weight of the cross makes itself felt. Some in the crowd want to see Jesus defeated; they can't wait for the moment when the nails will be pounded into Him. Others find cruel satisfaction in witnessing the violence and the rantings of those engulfed in bitter passions. Still others are drawn more by the One who carries the cross than by the cross itself—drawn by His face, His gaze, the way His hands grip the instrument of His condemnation. On one side—dark turmoil. On the other —silent compassion, a sentiment that enables us to belong to the One whom compassion cherishes, consoles, and sustains.

Woman is the privileged guardian of life, which has its source in God (see Gen 3:20). So mothers surround the Lord with their soft, caring, beautiful, and anguished faces. They mourn Him as one mourns an only son, as one weeps for a firstborn (see Zech 12:10). Christ, however, directs their compassion away from Himself. He tells the women to cry for themselves and their children

because their generation has closed itself to God's love. Through the pain of childbirth a fruit is born that delights the mother. But sin causes that life, linked to the blood of the mother, to die. The mothers of Jerusalem discern that the Blood that gives life, the Blood that never dies, is about to be poured out, and they desire this life-giving Blood for their children. Otherwise, blessed are the sterile and the wombs that never bore (see Lk 23:29).

It seems that the man of God experiences three births: the first, from the womb to creation; the second, from slavery to freedom, from being a man to being a son of God—something which happens through the grace of Baptism; while the third birth happens when one is reborn of his own free will from a carnal way of life to a spiritual one, and he himself becomes a womb that gives birth through total self-renunciation (see Phil 2:7).

Philoxenus of Mabbug,
Homily 9

And I will pour out a spirit of compassion and supplication on the house of David and the inhabitants of Jerusalem, so that, when they look on the one whom they have pierced, they shall mourn for him, as one mourns for an only child, and weep bitterly over him, as one weeps over a firstborn. On that day the mourning in Jerusalem will be as great as the mourning for Hadad-rimmon in the plain of Megiddo. The land shall mourn, each family by itself.

Zechariah 12:10–12

Let me share with you his pain,
who for all my sins was slain,
who for me in torment died.

NINTH STATION

JESUS FALLS THE THIRD TIME

℣. We adore you, O Christ,
and we bless you.

℟. Because by your holy cross
you have redeemed the world.

Jesus answered them, "The hour has come for the
Son of Man to be glorified. Very truly, I tell you,
unless a grain of wheat falls into the earth and
dies, it remains just a single grain; but if it dies, it
bears much fruit. Those who love their life lose
it, and those who hate their life in this world will
keep it for eternal life. Whoever serves me must
follow me, and where I am, there will my servant
be also. Whoever serves me, the Father will
honor."

John 12:23–26

When Jesus falls the third time, the cross covers Him almost completely. The weight of sin bears down on Him. The space between evil and the earth—humble witness and victim—shrinks more and more, so that one is terrified at the possibility of sin exterminating life. Sin manages to convert a garden into a lifeless wasteland (see Jer 17:6). The Bible begins its revelation in a garden overflowing with life and ends with a magnificent city adorned as a bride. Between Eden and the heavenly Jerusalem, the pride of sin and evil emerges and tries to vanquish, usurp, and bury humanity. And Christ allows Himself to be overpowered. He lets himself be crushed, thus accomplishing the work of the redemption. His face remains the only space of life. In His countenance all those overwhelmed by evil and sin are kneaded together so as to enter into Him, in that love which, even though it be killed, rises again and walks (see 1 Cor 5:6–8). Just by the glimpse of light emanating from the Redeemer's face, a new exodus of the redeemed who will populate that heavenly city begins anew.

God did not recreate us out of the same material with which he created us. Then, he made the first man taking mud from the earth, but for the second creation he gives his own body and in order to reanimate life in us . . . he pours out his very blood in the heart of the communicant, making his own life spring up within. Once he breathed a breath of life, now he communicates his own Spirit.

Nicholas Cabasilas,
The Life in Christ

Every member of your most holy body endured disgrace for our sakes: your head, the thorns; your face, the spitting; your cheeks, the blows; your mouth, the taste of gall mixed with vinegar; your ears, the impious blasphemies; your shoulders, the cloak of derision; your back, the scourging; your hand, the reed; your entire body stretching on the cross; your hands and feet, the nails; your side, the spear.

O you who suffered for us and freed us from our passions, you who in your love for mankind

stooped down to us in self-abasement and raised
us up, O almighty Savior, have mercy on us.

Byzantine liturgy,
Office of the Holy Passion

Save me, O God,
>   for the waters have come up to my neck.
I sink in deep mire,
>   where there is no foothold;
I have come into deep waters,
>   and the flood sweeps over me.
I am weary with my crying;
>   my throat is parched.
My eyes grow dim
>   with waiting for my God.

Psalm 69:1–3

O my Mother, fount of love,
touch my spirit from above;
make my heart with yours accord.

TENTH STATION

JESUS IS STRIPPED OF HIS CLOTHING

℣. We adore you, O Christ,
and we bless you.

℟. Because by your holy cross
you have redeemed the world.

[T]he night is far gone, the day is near. Let us then lay aside the works of darkness and put on the armor of light; let us live honorably as in the day, not in reveling and drunkenness, not in debauchery and licentiousness, not in quarreling and jealousy. Instead, put on the Lord Jesus Christ, and make no provision for the flesh, to gratify its desires.

Romans 13:12–14

Created in the image of God and placed in the Garden of Eden, Adam and Eve were clothed in glory. They were not naked. Their nearness to God and their powerful likeness to the Creator kept them in the presence of Divine Light. But after sin, they recognize their nakedness. The light is gone and, in the shock of nightfall, they discover that they are wounded and can die. The fear of disappearing and being vanquished becomes a constant presence in their hearts. Their nakedness expresses humanity's new identity, marked by sin and its wages: death. Fear for self is born and, with it, the urgency to save one's self. One has to steal what was lost: life. However, this anxiety always leads to failure.

The Lord allows Himself to be placed in this situation and takes the fear of humanity upon Himself. He hands Himself over, completely submissive, without defenses, and readily accepts humiliation. The naked Christ reminds us that in Him, sinful humanity is stripped of the old man. He who did not know sin was treated as sin so that humanity could be re-clothed with light and glory.

He, stripped and vulnerable, clothes us anew and saves us (see Rom 13:14; Gal 3:27; 2 Cor 5:4).

Having stripped yourselves [in Baptism], you were naked; thus imitating Christ, who was naked on the cross, and by his nakedness stripped himself of principalities and powers, and openly triumphed over them on the tree. For since the powers of evil lived in your body, you may no longer wear the old garment; I am not talking about that visible garment, but the old man, which is being corrupted through its deceptive lusts.

Cyril of Jerusalem,
Second Mystagogical Catechesis

Through your divestment on the wood,
in exchange for the nakedness of the first man,
cover me with glory
on the day of the universal judgment.

Nerses Shnorhali,
Jesus, the Son

For dogs are all around me;
a company of evildoers encircles me.
My hands and feet have shriveled;
I can count all my bones.
They stare and gloat over me;
they divide my clothes among themselves,
and for my clothing they cast lots.

Psalm 22:16–18

Make me feel as you have felt,
make my soul to glow and melt,
with the love of Christ, my Lord.

ELEVENTH STATION

JESUS IS NAILED TO THE CROSS

℣. We adore you, O Christ,
   and we bless you.

℟. Because by your holy cross
   you have redeemed the world.

When they came to the place that is called The Skull, they crucified Jesus there with the criminals, one on his right and one on his left. . . . And the people stood by, watching; but the leaders scoffed at him, saying, "He saved others; let him save himself if he is the Messiah of God, his chosen one!"

Luke 23:33, 35

To the disgrace of humanity, a man's hand takes the foot of the Son of God and nails it to the cross. The nailed feet signify the end of liberty. The nailed One is no longer free. Yet Christ repeatedly maintained that He came into the world to be handed over to men (see Mk 10:33). Paul affirmed that Jesus gave Himself up for us when we were still at enmity with God (see Rom 5:10). Jesus' trusting gift of self demonstrates to us the greatness of God's love. Freedom inhabits love from within, like salt, without which food would spoil. Love renders one free enough to become an object in the violent hands of those who are evil, those who coerce, confine, and kill. Christ Himself said that no one takes His life from Him, because He Himself offered it (see Jn 10:18). Love for the Father whom He wants to obey in everything coincides with the violent hands of those who crucify Him—love for the Father and for the people. Sinners either fix their eyes on sin with greed and passion, or they are nailed to sin by a tragic sense of guilt. Now God lets Himself be nailed to that evil, to that sin, to that tree on which man—in the

beginning, in temptation—set his sight. All this so that man would encounter Him and discover that He is not an object but a person with an identity who possesses the freedom of love.

Christ unites the created and uncreated reality in love—O wonder of the Divine tenderness and friendship toward us!—and shows us that through grace the two realities are one thing. The whole world enters completely in the total God and becomes all that God is, with the exception of his nature; in place of itself it now receives the complete God.

Maximus the Confessor,
Ambigua

I gave my back to those who struck me,
  and my cheeks to those who pulled out the
   beard;
I did not hide my face
  from insult and spitting.
The Lord GOD helps me;
  therefore I have not been disgraced;

therefore I have set my face like flint,
    and I know that I shall not be put to shame.

Isaiah 50:6–7

Holy Mother, pierce me through,
in my heart each wound renew,
of my Savior crucified.

TWELFTH STATION

JESUS DIES
ON THE CROSS

℣. We adore you, O Christ,
and we bless you.

℟. Because by your holy cross
you have redeemed the world.

Since it was the day of Preparation, the Jews did not want the bodies left on the cross during the sabbath, especially because that sabbath was a day of great solemnity. So they asked Pilate to have the legs of the crucified men broken and the bodies removed. Then the soldiers came and broke the legs of the first and of the other who had been crucified with him. But when they came to Jesus and saw that he was already dead, they did not break his legs. Instead, one of the soldiers pierced his side with a spear, and at once blood and water came out. (He who saw this has testified so that you also may believe. His testimony is true, and he knows that he tells the truth.) These things occurred so that the scripture might be fulfilled, "None of his bones shall be broken." And again another passage of scripture says, "They will look on the one whom they have pierced."

John 19:31–37

———————— ◦◄►◦ ————————

Humanity finally obtained what it wanted—to kill Christ. And God brought about what He wanted—to conquer sin and the evil of the world. But to achieve this Christ had to die. And to die He surrenders to the consequences of sin. While He lies under this evil and takes it on Himself, He is lifted up as Moses lifted the bronze serpent (see Num 21:9).

Christ dies only so that death might think it has won. But in reality He has absorbed everything, letting it burn in the Father's love. Jesus died in our place so that death for us is no longer the

end of everything. The grace has been given to us to die with Him in Baptism in a death similar to His. Therefore death is no longer definitive; it is entirely within time and behind us. Ahead of us lies that which we have already experienced in Baptism: the "little resurrection"; and in the Eucharist: eternal life.

The gaze of Christ crucified is the gaze of God's relentless love for us. Christ gave Himself up because He loved us so much that He considered us worthy of His trust. We handed over our own death so that He should die and we should remain alive. The image of Christ on the cross, pierced by a lance, is the image of God that we have fashioned with our hands, through God's grace. We fashioned His death, but He washed us in His Blood, giving us life. Christ slept in death only for a moment, while immediately, from the side of the New Adam, the new humanity was born.

Christ slept on the cross, and Baptism flowed out
   from him;
the Bridegroom slept, and his side was pierced in his
   sleep,
giving birth to the Bride, as happened with Adam and
   Eve, the archetype.
. . . The silence of the sleep of death fell upon him on
   the cross,
and from him came forth the Mother (Baptism) who
   gives birth to all spiritual beings;
the Lord of Adam produced the New Eve in his sleep
to serve as mother of the children of Adam in the
   place of Eve—
water and blood to fashion spiritual children,
flowing from the side of the Living One who died to
   give life to Adam.

> Jacob of Serugh,
> *Homilies*

Therefore I will allot him a portion with the great,
      and he shall divide the spoil with the strong;
because he poured out himself to death,
      and was numbered with the transgressors;

yet he bore the sin of many,
  and made intercession for the transgressors.

Isaiah 53:12

For the sins of his own nation,
she saw him hang in desolation
till his spirit forth he sent.

Thirteenth Station

JESUS IS TAKEN DOWN FROM THE CROSS

℣. We adore you, O Christ,
and we bless you.

℟. Because by your holy cross
you have redeemed the world.

After these things, Joseph of Arimathea, who was a disciple of Jesus, though a secret one because of his fear of the Jews, asked Pilate to let him take away the body of Jesus. Pilate gave him permission; so he came and removed his body. Nicodemus, who had at first come to Jesus by night, also came, bringing a mixture of myrrh and aloes, weighing about a hundred pounds. They took the body of Jesus and wrapped it with the spices in linen cloths, according to the burial custom of the Jews. Now there was a garden in the place where he was crucified, and in the garden there was a new tomb in which no one had ever been laid. And so, because it was the Jewish day of Preparation, and the tomb was nearby, they laid Jesus there.

John 19:38–42

Present in the oldest of icons, this scene is the first gesture of tenderness on the part of redeemed humanity toward God, toward the dead body of Christ. After Jesus' sacrifice, humanity is finally capable of loving, because it is redeemed. Sin has been conquered; the law of death has been overcome. Earlier, the women of Jerusalem had approached Jesus with a look of compassion; now a man, Joseph of Arimathea, does the same. All of humanity is drawn to Him. Joseph carries Jesus' body just as in the beginning the Lord carried humanity. He cradles the body of Jesus, but in reality he is the one enfolded in the love of God. It is not we who have loved God, but He who has loved us (see 1 Jn 4:10).

The perfume used to anoint Christ's body has a nuptial significance; finally God and humanity can meet and exchange love. Now Love is loved. The world does not recognize Christ, but it can see those who have been touched by the Lord's death and resurrection. All our fears, anger, rancor, resentments, and deaths are gathered into His death. The one who carries within the death of Christ is freed from death and is able to love because he or she no longer worries about oneself. Those who see compassion and tenderness in these witnesses recognize Christ. These are the ones who become the body of the Lord, the body that lets His love shine through to the world.

The Sun of Justice was taken down from the arms of the cross. The Church embraced him and kissed his wounds, saying, "Our Lord, have mercy on your body lying in corruption in Sheol, where Death now reigns." And He said: "Have patience, beloved Church, because I will get up, I

will rise and my friends, all those who acknowl-
edge my passion, will rejoice in me, alleluia."
[. . .] Living One, Creator of life and Giver of
life.

Lord, with the fragrant incense of your
sweetness and the delicious smell of your goodness you descended in Sheol and you breathed
into it the resurrection and the life. With the
sweet incense of your death you destroyed death
and took away its treasures, and with your new
life you have cheered those who lingered in Sheol
and you have delighted them with the good news
of the resurrection.

Syro-Antiochian liturgy,
Holy Saturday Evening Prayer

By a perversion of justice he was taken away.
    Who could have imagined his future?
For he was cut off from the land of the living,
    stricken for the transgression of my people.
They made his grave with the wicked
    and his tomb with the rich,
although he had done no violence,
    and there was no deceit in his mouth.

Isaiah 53:8–9

Let me mingle tears with you,
mourning him who mourned for me
all the days that I may live.

FOURTEENTH STATION

JESUS' BODY
IS PLACED IN
THE SEPULCHER

℣. We adore you, O Christ,
and we bless you.

℟. Because by your holy cross
you have redeemed the world.

Do you not know that all of us who have been
baptized into Christ Jesus were baptized into his
death? Therefore we have been buried with him
by baptism into death, so that, just as Christ was
raised from the dead by the glory of the Father,
so we too might walk in newness of life. For if we
have been united with him in a death like his, we
will certainly be united with him in a resurrection like his. We know that our old self was
crucified with him so that the body of sin might
be destroyed, and we might no longer be enslaved
to sin.

Romans 6:3–6

Christ is dead. It is as if He were resting, as if a deep sleep had fallen upon Him, but now He is without the weight of the cross. This scene seems removed from life and history; no crowd applauds as when He entered Jerusalem, no one accompanies Him as in Gethsemane, no spectators jeer as on Calvary. But between the obscurity of the dark and the dawn of Easter day, Christ is supremely active: He descends into the grave to search for Adam and Eve and to bring back risen humanity to the Father. For those who live in Sheol, where everything is in shadows, light is critical, as is the hope of day. Someone has to come; He is about to arrive, to manifest Himself. . . .

In Baptism we were pulled out of the grave. Our life has been marked by Someone who touched our dead body with love, gave us life again, clothed us in a new robe, slipped a ring on our finger and sat us at table (see Lk 15:22). Yet we often still find ourselves in the darkness, like the buried grain of wheat that has already died but hasn't yet sent up its first shoots. In these long hours before dawn, we are

comforted by the expectation of the One who has
already come to rescue us.

[Death speaks:] The death of Jesus torments me;
I would rather have left him alive: it would have been
    better for me than his death.
Here is a man whose death I find detestable;
in the death of every other person I rejoice, but his
    death haunts me
and I wait for him to come back to life:
during his lifetime he revived and brought back to life
    three that were dead.
But now, through his death, all the dead who have
    come back to life
trample me down at the gates of Hell when I try to
    restrain them. [. . .]

[Ephrem's prayer:] Jesus, King, grant my request,
and with my request take to yourself a pledge,
even Adam, in whom all the dead are buried—
just as, when I received him, all the living were
    contained.
The first pledge I have given you, the body of Adam.
Ascend now, and reign over all,

and when I hear the sound of your trumpet,
with my very own hands I will conduct the dead to
   your coming.

Ephrem the Syrian,
The Nisibene Hymns

What shall I return to the LORD
      for all his bounty to me?
I will lift up the cup of salvation
      and call on the name of the LORD,
I will pay my vows to the LORD
      in the presence of all his people.
Precious in the sight of the LORD
      is the death of his faithful ones.

Psalm 116:12–15

While my body here decays,
may my soul your goodness praise,
safe in paradise with you. Amen.

Pauline
BOOKS & MEDIA

A mission of the Daughters of St. Paul

As apostles of Jesus Christ, evangelizing today's world:

We are CALLED to holiness
by God's living Word and Eucharist.

We COMMUNICATE the Gospel message
through our lives and through all
available forms of media.

We SERVE the Church
by responding to the hopes and needs
of all people with the Word of God,
in the spirit of St. Paul.

For more information visit our web site:
www.pauline.org.

BOOKS & MEDIA

The Daughters of St. Paul operate book and media centers at the following addresses. Visit, call, or write the one nearest you today, or find us at www.paulinestore.org.

CALIFORNIA
3908 Sepulveda Blvd, Culver City, CA 90230   310-397-8676
3250 Middlefield Road, Menlo Park, CA 94025   650-369-4230

FLORIDA
145 S.W. 107th Avenue, Miami, FL 33174   305-559-6715

HAWAII
1143 Bishop Street, Honolulu, HI 96813   808-521-2731

ILLINOIS
172 North Michigan Avenue, Chicago, IL 60601   312-346-4228

LOUISIANA
4403 Veterans Memorial Blvd, Metairie, LA 70006   504-887-7631

MASSACHUSETTS
885 Providence Hwy, Dedham, MA 02026   781-326-5385

MISSOURI
9804 Watson Road, St. Louis, MO 63126   314-965-3512

NEW YORK
115 E. 29th Street, New York City, NY 10016   212-754-1110

SOUTH CAROLINA
243 King Street, Charleston, SC 29401   843-577-0175

TEXAS
No book center; for parish exhibits or outreach evangelization, contact: 210-569-0500, or SanAntonio@paulinemedia.com, or P.O. Box 761416, San Antonio, TX 78245

VIRGINIA
1025 King Street, Alexandria, VA 22314   703-549-3806

CANADA
3022 Dufferin Street, Toronto, ON M6B 3T5   416-781-9131